THE SUN

KU-680-188

Mary-Jane Wilkins
Consultant: Giles Sparrow, FRAS

Published in paperback in 2017 by Wayland

© 2017 Brown Bear Books Ltd

Wayland
An imprint of Hachette Children's Group
Part of Hodder & Stoughton
Carmelite House
50 Victoria Embankment
London EC4Y 0DZ
An Hachette UK Company
www.hachette.co.uk
www.hachettechildrens.co.uk

ISBN 978 1 5263 0288 5

Brown Bear Books Ltd
First Floor, 9–17 St. Albans Place
London N1 0NX

Author: Mary-Jane Wilkins
Consultant: Giles Sparrow, Fellow of the Royal
Astronomical Society
Picture Researcher: Clare Newman
Illustrations: Supriya Sahai
Designer: Melissa Roskell
Design Manager: Keith Davis
Editorial Director: Lindsey Lowe
Children's Publisher: Anne O'Daly

Printed in Malaysia

Websites
The website addresses (URLs) included in this
book were valid at the time of going to press.
However, it is possible that contents or addresses
may change following the publication of this
book. No responsibility for any such changes
can be accepted by either the author or the
Publisher.

Contents

What is the Sun?

The Sun is a star. It is a huge, shining ball of gas. The Sun sends out the heat and light we call sunshine.

Without the Sun, Earth would be a dark and cold place. Nothing could live here.

The Sun is 150 million km away from us. A jet plane would take 19 years to reach it!

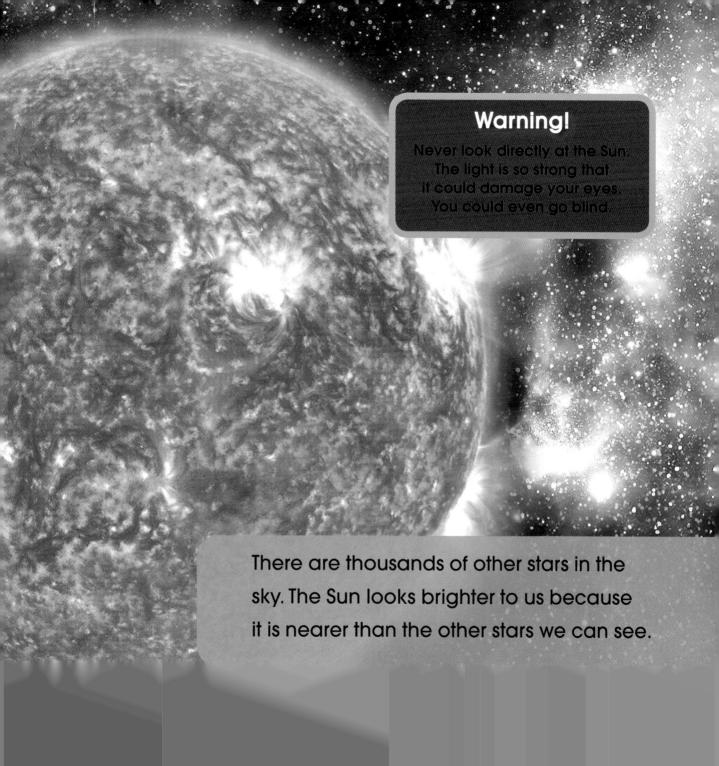

There are thousands of other stars in the sky. The Sun looks brighter to us because it is nearer than the other stars we can see.

The solar system

The Sun is in the middle of a group of eight planets. The planets circle around (or orbit) the Sun. Earth is one of them. The other planets are Mercury, Venus, Mars, Jupiter, Saturn, Uranus and Neptune.

Comets are lumps of rock and ice that move around the Sun.

Mars

Jupiter

Mercury

Venus

Earth

WOW!
The Sun is huge!
More than a million
Earths would fit inside it.

Earth's Moon

Dwarf planets also orbit the Sun. Pluto is a dwarf planet. Freezing comets and rocky asteroids travel around the Sun, too.

The Sun, the planets and other space objects make up the solar system.

Saturn

Uranus

Neptune

Pluto (dwarf planet)

Day and night

When there are no clouds in the sky, we see the Sun during the day. It disappears at night. We can watch the Sun rise at the start of a day. At night we see it disappear at sunset.

The Earth takes 24 hours, or one day, to spin all the way around once.

The sun rises and sets because the Earth turns, or rotates, like a spinning top. When the part of the Earth you live on faces the Sun, it is day. When your part of the Earth faces away from the Sun, it is night.

What is the Sun like?

The Sun is a giant ball of burning gas. Lots of explosions inside the Sun make the heat and light it gives out. The Sun looks like it's burning, but it's really exploding like a big bomb.

Dark spots on the Sun are called sunspots. The temperature is lower here.

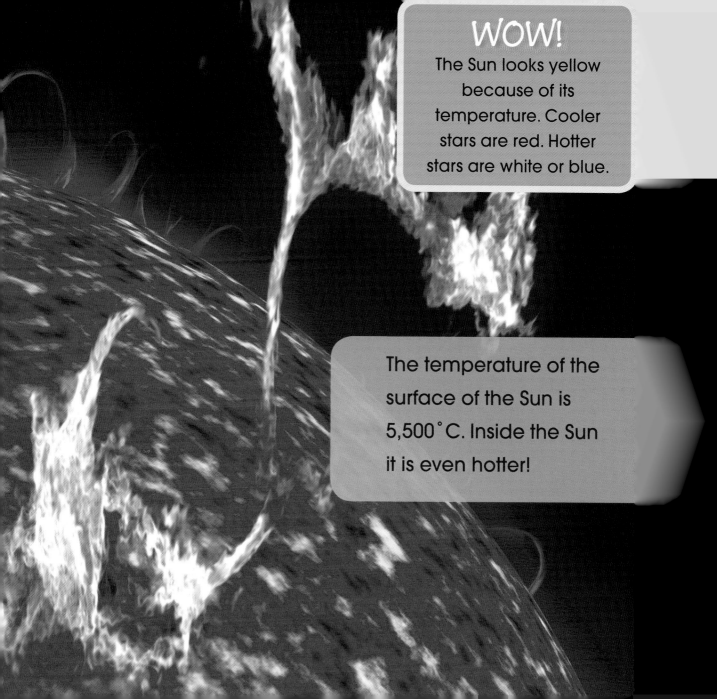

The solar wind

The Sun sends tiny specks called particles into space. This is the solar wind. It streams off the Sun at about 1.6 million kph.

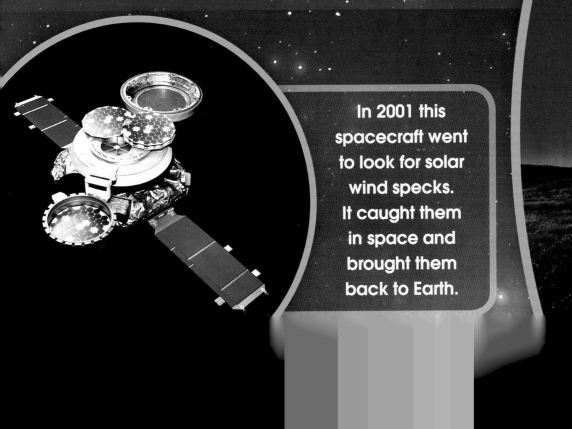

In 2001 this spacecraft went to look for solar wind specks. It caught them in space and brought them back to Earth.

When the solar wind goes past Earth's North or South Pole, it makes the air glow with colours. The solar wind fills the sky with red, blue, green and purple colours. These are called an aurora.

Storms on the Sun

The Sun looks like a yellow ball from Earth, but if you could see it up close it would seem different. There are lots of storms on the surface of the Sun.

Bright flashes on the Sun are called solar flares.

Sometimes big streams of gas burst away from the Sun. They can be bigger than Earth. Some of the gas falls back onto the Sun. The rest goes into space.

How do we know about the Sun?

We need to find out about the Sun, but it is so hot that humans could never visit it. So scientists study the Sun with space probes. The scientists look at storms on the Sun that might cause problems on Earth.

WOW!

The SOHO probe has been looking at the Sun for 19 years.

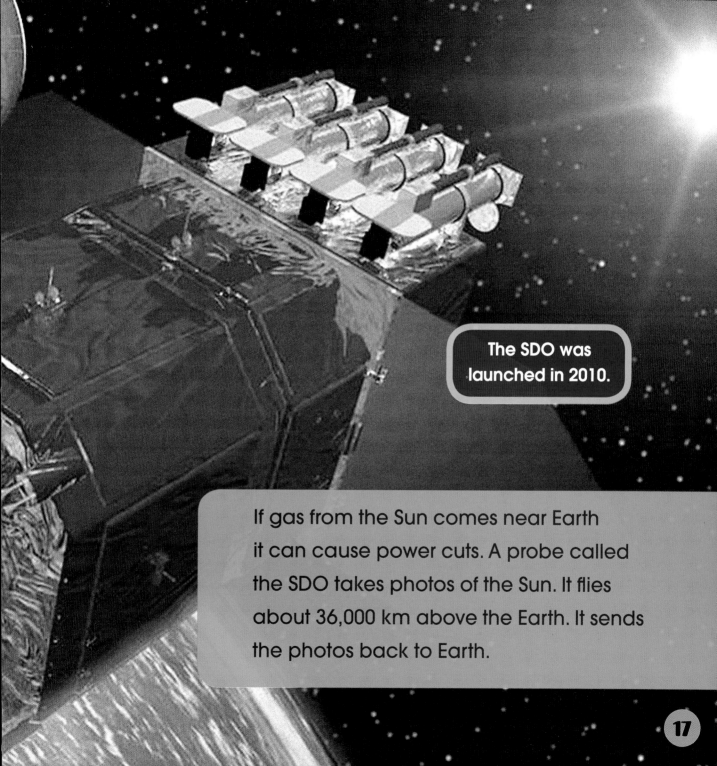

The SDO was launched in 2010.

If gas from the Sun comes near Earth it can cause power cuts. A probe called the SDO takes photos of the Sun. It flies about 36,000 km above the Earth. It sends the photos back to Earth.

The Sun and life on Earth

Without the Sun, there would be no life on Earth. The Sun gives Earth the light and warmth that plants need to grow. The plants are food for Earth's animals.

Most of Earth
is covered
in water.

Plants need water, too. If Earth was closer to the Sun, all the water on Earth would boil away. Earth is just the right distance from the Sun for plants to grow here.

Eclipses

Earth orbits the Sun. Our Moon orbits Earth. Sometimes the Moon goes between the Sun and Earth. Then the Moon blocks the Sun's light. This is called an eclipse. On Earth the sky goes dark.

The Moon blocks out part of the Sun in a partial eclipse.

Sometimes the Moon blocks out the Sun completely. This is a total eclipse (see below). In a partial eclipse the Moon just blocks out a bit of the Sun. It looks as though someone has taken a bite out of the Sun.

Make a sundial

What you need
Paper plate
Sharp pencil
Plastic drinking straw

Modelling clay
Ruler
Paint, to decorate your sundial

What to do

1. Make a hole in the centre of the plate with the pencil. Push the straw through the hole. Put a ball of modelling clay at the bottom of the straw.

2. Put the plate in a sunny spot outside.

3. At noon, draw a line on the plate along the straw's shadow. Write 12 on the plate at the end of the line.

4. Do the same one hour later, and write 1 on the plate.

5. Carry on each hour, marking numbers. Finish your sundial next morning. Use it to tell the time on a sunny day.

Useful words

asteroid
A big rock that orbits the Sun. An asteroid can be just a few metres across or hundreds of kilometres wide.

comet
A ball of rock, dust and ice that orbits the Sun.

eclipse
There is an eclipse when an object in space passes in front of another one and hides it. In a solar eclipse, the Moon blocks the light of the Sun.

orbit
To move around another object.

planet
A large object in space that orbits the Sun.

rotate
To spin like a top.

solar
To do with the Sun.

Sun
The star at the centre of the solar system.

Find out more

Websites
www.kidsastronomy.com/
our_sun.htm

www.planetsforkids.org/
star-sun.html

http://ngkids.co.uk/science-
and-nature/universe-facts

Books
Fact Cat Sun, Alice Harman
(Wayland, 2015)

First Fabulous Facts Space,
Anita Ganeri (Ladybird, 2014)

Our Sun (Space), Ian Graham
(Franklin Watts, 2016)

Index